This book belongs to

....

To my children, Blake and Ocean — M.H.

For every child — D.E.

First published 2022 by Macmillan Children's Books
an imprint of Pan Macmillan
The Smithson, 6 Briset Street, London EC1M 5NR
EU representative: Macmillan Publishers Ireland Ltd, 1st Floor,
The Liffey Trust Centre, 117-126 Sheriff Street Upper, Dublin 1, D01 YC43

www.panmacmillan.com

ISBN: 978-1-5290-8388-0

Text copyright © Marvyn Harrison 2022
Illustration copyright © Diane Ewen 2022
Photograph of Marvyn Harrison by Henry Robinson

With thanks to Laura Henry-Allain MBE for her help with this book

1 3 5 7 9 8 6 4 2

A CIP catalogue record for this book is available
from the British Library.

Printed in China

FSC
www.fsc.org
MIX
Paper from
responsible sources
FSC® C116313

Marvyn
Harrison

Diane
Ewen

Macmillan Children's Books

Every morning, we look into the mirror with Daddy. Together, we say words to help us feel proud and brave, powerful and strong . . .

On Monday, we start the week with . . .

I AM BRAVE!

I play on the big slide.

My brother and I are superheroes.

Monster

I'm not scared of monsters!

I am brave when I try something new.

On Tuesday, we boost our brains with . . .

I can learn to count.

I can read my books.

I can get dressed
all by myself.

I can even make
gooey potions!

On Wednesday,
we stand tall and shout . . .

I can help with
the shopping.

I AM
STRONG!

can swing on the climbing frame.

I can tug on the rope.

If I am sick,
I rest till I feel
strong again.

On Thursday,
we smile and say . . .

I AM KIND!

I share my food with my sister.

I look after Stormzy.

I care about my world.

I hug my friends when they are sad.

On Friday,
we jump out of bed and cheer . . .

I brush my teeth
with a great big smile

I jump in the puddles.

I build a giant tower.

I am happy inside and out.

On Saturday, our family is all together. It's time to shout . . .

I AM LOVING!

I love Mummy.

I love Daddy.

I love my sister.

I love Granny
and Grandpa

. . . and I also
love ME!

On Sunday, we always look our best because . . .

WE ARE BEAUTIFUL!

We have a big bath.

We comb our hair.

We dress up to go to the shops.

We are beautiful even when we sleep.

Every week, we choose words to help us feel
BRAVE, BEAUTIFUL and POWERFUL.

Say them out LOUD
with us . . .

He
gr
W

I AM BRAVE!

I AM BEAUTIFUL!

I AM POWERFUL!

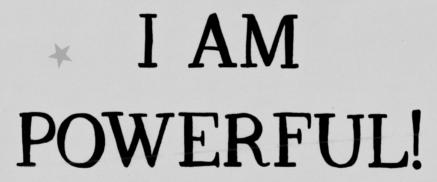

NOTES FOR PARENTS AND CARERS

Marvyn Harrison

Each and every child is special, and it is important that we tell them so every day.

The way I do this with my children is to stand in front of a mirror and shout loudly all the best things about ourselves. We call this 'mirror talk' or 'affirmations'.

There are many examples of affirmations in this book – why not try them with your own child? Just make sure they say them LOUD and have a big smile on their face! Affirmations help a child to have a strong and healthy mind for when they grow up.

Here are some suggestions to get you started . . .

Say the affirmations in front of a mirror.
This allows your child to see themselves while together you celebrate all of their best parts.

Encourage your child to look at their reflection.
For many children, eye contact is great for developing confidence.

Say the affirmations loudly.
This helps your child to remember just how amazing they are!

Make it fun!
Playful poses and funny voices can really help your child to stay focused throughout.

Let your child choose their own affirmations.
This makes the activity much more personal and reflects how they feel in the moment.

You might like to end with a hug.
This can help your child to feel safe and loved.

My philosophy on affirmations is that it's easier to raise healthy children than it is to fix unhealthy adults.

Just as regular exercise and a balanced diet set up strong patterns for good physical health, so can practising affirmations lead to better mental health. Saying affirmations regularly helps children to understand and communicate their feelings. It also boosts their self-esteem, helping to establish positive ideas about themselves that they can carry forward as grown-ups.

There are many situations in life that we cannot control but affirmations help us to control how we feel about **ourselves**.

I hope you and your child have fun discovering the words that help you to feel your best.

Marvyn

DOPE BLACK DADS

Dope Black Dads is an online community that encourages healthy discussions about race, masculinity, mental health and male parenting. The group has created an award-winning podcast which candidly speaks on the experiences and stories of its members, with the goal of helping everyone to better understand what it is like to be a Black father and to improve the outcomes for our families.

For more information, visit:
www.dopeblack.org/dopeblackdads

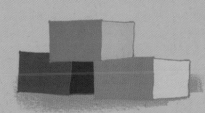

Reading Together

This book has been specifically created for preschool children. Reading books together can give a child a head start at nursery and school by helping them to develop their communication skills and imagination. There are many ways you and your child can make the most of the books you share . . .

- You could read *I Love Me!* from start to finish in one sitting, or dip in and out by returning to your child's favourite pages!

- The story follows the characters from Monday through to Sunday, to help with learning the days of the week and family routines.

- The book also encourages children to talk about themselves, and express their thoughts and feelings.

- Sharing books is a wonderful way to spend quality time with your child, and provides a starting point for all sorts of new conversations. This in turn aids learning by developing listening, concentration and vocabulary skills.

When you read this book together, you could talk to your child about . . .

. . . their opinions and experiences. Why is it 'brave' to try something new, and why is it 'kind' to share snacks with your sister? Can your child think of any **moments or events that made them feel strong, clever or loving?**

. . . the words the characters use to talk about themselves. Why is it important to be kind or loving or brave? **Which positive words would your child use to describe themselves?** How would they describe the people around them?

. . . the activities they do in a typical week. **What happens in their daily routine,** like getting dressed and brushing their teeth? Which days of the week have special events, like visiting grandparents or going to a swimming club?

. . . things to spot. Try using the book to play a game of I-spy. How many times can your child spot Stormzy the dog? Or the little girl's favourite teddy bear? **Choose different things for your child to find.** Then see if they can find some things for you to spot too!

1 Week Loan

This book is due for return on or before the last date shown below

University of Cumbria

Health
risk management

Dr Tony Boyle

This book is printed on chlorine-free, acid-free stock produced from woodpulp originating from managed, sustainable plantations. The paper and board are recyclable and biodegradable.

First published 2000
Second edition 2002, revised 2005 (twice)
Third edition 2008, revised 2010, 2012

© Dr Tony Boyle 2012
Printed in England by the Lavenham Press Limited

ISBN-13: 978 0 901357 41 0

Published by IOSH Services Limited
The Grange
Highfield Drive
Wigston
Leicestershire
LE18 1NN
UK
t +44 (0)116 257 3100
f +44 (0)116 257 3101
www.iosh.co.uk